TABLE OF CONTENTS

25 elderflower heads
3 lemons sliced
1 kg sugar

Dilute with soda to
taste. Add to fruit
salads or make
ice lollies.

Elderflower Lemonade

Make sure there are no insects in flowers. Place heads in large bowl with lemon slices. Bring 1.5 litres water to boil and pour over flowers. Cover & leave overnight to infuse. Strain liquid through muslin & pour into saucepan. Add sugar. Heat gently to dissolve sugar, bring to simmer for 2 mins. Use funnel to pour syrup into sterilised bottles.

2 litres cider 6 cloves 4 star anise 2 cinnamon stick 2 orange 1 apple 1 pomegranate, juice & seeds 5 tbs sugar

Slice apple and one of the oranges thinly. Jiuce the other orange & add to large pan with cider on low heat and

let it warm through for a few minutes. Add all the spices and let it gentley simmer 10 mins. Add sugar to taste.

Ladle into glasses or mugs and serve warm.

3 cups water 4 cups sugar
1 cup red roses tightly packed

Makes a delicate & aromatic syrup
perfect for drinks & desserts

Rose

Rinse rose petals & remove white base. Combine sugar & water in saucepan, bring to boil, stirring constantly to dissolve sugar. Add rose petals & simmer for 20 mins. Cool for 3 hours. Strain through muslin cloth & store in clean airtight bottle

Syrup

Rose Margarita

1 ounce tequila

1 ounce triple sec

1 ounce rose syrup

1 ounce fresh lime juice

Pour ingrediants into shaker with ice.

Shake for 1 minute & pour into glass

5 cups seedless watermelon

10 oz Gin

1 large English cucumber peeled & cubed

20 mint leaves

Ice cubes

2 tbsp honey

¼ cup fresh lime juice

mint, watermelon & cucumber cooler

In a blender, combine the watermelon, cucumber, mint. Pour into a sieve & strain out the liquid. In a small bowl stir together lime juice and honey. Add to watermelon and cucumber juices, along with gin. Fill four glasses with ice and top each with cocktail. Garnish with cucumber slices (omit gin for mocktail)

Roasted Asparagus with Bacon & Eggs

Preheat oven to 375°C F. Heat olive oil in skillet over medium heat. Fry bacon until crisp 5-6 mins. Transfer to paper lined plate. Drain excess fat. Add asparagus to skillet & transfer to oven for 8-10 mins. Carefully crack eggs onto asparagus. Return to oven 4-5 mins. Return bacon to pan & transfer to warm plate.

Place each corn on a piece of aluminum foil.

Add 1 tsp butter, season with salt and pepper and 1 ice cube.

Wrap each securely, twisting ends – handles for turning.

(cool) grilled
CORN ON THE COb

Grill corn over medium heat for 10 mins on each side.

Inspired by Salli Swindell 'the 100 day project'

Great for summer Barbecues- corn cooks in its own steam !

BUTTER

courgettes

parsnips

beetroots

carrots

olive oil

salt

Autumn Vegetable Crisps

Thinly slice vegetables
Mix with a few drops of olive oil
Spread on baking paper in single layer
Bake at 160°c for 20mins
(50 mins for courgettes)
When cooled sprinkle
with salt

Use griddled AUBERGINE in salads

Slice BANANAS and freeze Whiz in blender till smooth

Make CHERRY compot with sugar and splash of water

Peel DAIKON into strips and serve in oriental salad

Poach EGGS serve on toast with avacdo

Whiz KIWI banana blueberry and yogurt

Toss LEMON juice with minced garlic and pasta

Saute MUSHROOMS with shallots and serve on toast

Poach QUINCE with honey and vanilla

Pickle sliced RADISH in apple cider vinegar with chilli flakes

Stir fry SPINICH with garlic and tofu

Simply peel TANGERINE

A

Fruit and Vegetables

Toss FIGS with pasta pancetta and cream

Mix cooked GOOSEBerries with cream yogurt and sugar

Whiz HAZELNUTS with cacao powder and dried figs for brownies

Wrap black beans and feta in ICEBERG LETTUCE

Add JALAPENO to pineapple salsa

Marinade OLIVES with chili garlic and feta cheese

Whiz NECTARINES with yogurt and banana in smoothie

Mix PAPAYA to exotic fruit salad

Toss SWEET POTATO with smoked paprika

simple ways to serve

Bury VANILLA BEAN in jar of sugar

Suggestions for UGLI fruit

Add WATERCRESS to sandwiches

Make soup with ZUCCHINI beans tomatoes and leeks

FUTO-MAKI
thick roll sushi

1 nori sheet
5oz cooked sushi rice
3-4 fillings eg. omlette avocado cucumber & carrot batons

Its much easier to make than it looks &
kids love to add their own fillings—makes 8

Cover mat tightly with cling film. Place nori
on sushi mat.

Roll the mat over, press ingredients in, to
keep roll firm

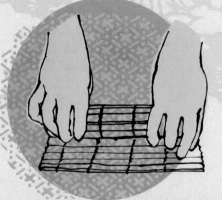

With the mat covering the roll press all
round to make roll firm

2

Use moist fingers to spread rice over nori sheet

3

Arrange the filling along the centre

6

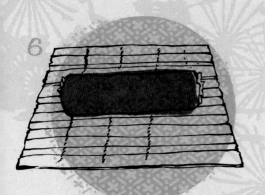

You now have a cylindrical roll

7

Place roll on chopping board, cut roll
in half then half again until you have 8

8

Herb Infused Oils

Use herb flavoured oils to dress salads or give soups a lift

rosemary & peppercorns

oregano & garlic

basil & thyme

Heat 1½ pint olive oil gently in a pan. Lightly bruise herbs & add to sterilized jar or bottle with spices (if using) Pour warm oil into jar then seal. Oil will be ready in 2-3 weeks.

sage & lemon

thyme & chilli

coriander & fennel

PEAR WALNUT

3 tbsp balsamic vinegar. 3 tbsp olive oil. 1 tsp honey. salt & pepper to taste. 50g walnuts. 1 bunch rocket leaves. 1 head lettuce torn. 2 pears, cored and sliced. 100g feta cheese

& Feta SALAD

Whisk the vinegar, oil, honey, salt and pepper together. Lightly toast walnuts in frying pan over medium heat. In a large bowl, mix the walnuts, lettuce, rocket and pears. Toss with the dressing to coat. Sprinkle with feta cheese to serve.

Butternut Squash
& CARROT SOUP

In a large pan fry the onions in oil until translucent and soft...Add squash and carrots and stir cooking for 5 minutes...Add thyme and season well with salt and freshly ground black pepper...Pour over stock and bring to boil...Allow to simmer for 30 minutes or until vegetables are cooked...Remove from heat and allow to cool...using a hand blender or a liquidiser blend to a smooth soup...Divide soup into bowls and serve with a dollop of creme fraiche...

2 onions chopped
1tbsp sunflower oil
1 butternut squash peeled and diced
4 carrots peeled and sliced
2 sprigs fresh thyme leaves only
Salt and fresh black pepper
1.5 litres hot vegetable stock

1 tablespoon olive oil
1 cup carrots, scrubbed, 1/4-inch dice
2 cups Spanish onions, 1/4-inch dice
1/4 cup celery, minced
2 tablespoons garlic, minced
2 cups oyster mushrooms, quartered
2 cups assorted wild mushrooms
cut into 1/2-inch pieces
1 cup dry sherry
1 cup dried porcini mushrooms
1 quart chicken stock or vegetable stock
Pinch chopped fresh sage
Salt and pepper

In a large saucepan, heat the olive oil over high heat, then add the carrots, onions, and celery. Sauté the mixture for 5 minutes.

Add the garlic, the oyster and wild mushrooms, and continue to sauté the mixture for 5 minute. Immediately deglaze the pan with the sherry, and then bring to a boil for 1 minute.

Add the dried porcini and stock. Bring to a boil, decrease the heat to low, then simmer until the stew reaches the desired consistency. Swirl in the sage, and then remove from the heat. Season with the salt and pepper.

1 (1/4 ounce) packet active dry yeast
1 tbsp organic honey
11/2 cups warm water
2 tsp natural sea salt
4 -4 1/2 cups all-purpose flour

Easy Baguette

Place the yeast, honey and warm water in large
bowl and stand for 5 mins. In a separate bowl,
whisk together the salt and the flour then add
to yeast mixture & stir. Turn out onto a lightly
floured work surface. Knead with floured hands
until dough is smooth and elastic, about 5-7
minutes. Add a little flour to prevent dough
from sticking.

Place in an oiled bowl, cover with plasticwrap and leave to rise until doubled, about 1 1/2 hours. Preheat oven to 400F degrees. Gently punch dough down to deflate it. Shape into two oblong baguettes. Dust tops lightly with flour and place on a lightly greased baking sheet, let rise uncovered for 30 minutes. Use a serrated knife to cut 3-5 small diagonal slits across the tops of the baguettes, and lightly sprinkle with cool water.Bake in the middle of oven for 25-30 minutes, until golden. Transfer to a rack to cool. Enjoy with a variety of cheeses and cold meats.

Asparagus with mustard seeds and fresh dill

Radish with fennel seeds and garlic clove

Cucumber with bay leaf and allspice

Carrorts with star anise and dill seeds

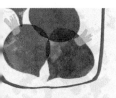

Mushrooms with peppercorns and thyme

Chili peppers with cinnamon and bay leaf

Green beans with fennel and chili flakes

Tomatoes with cloves and coriander

Preserve & PICKLE

BASIC SWEET PICKLE BRINE Combine 3 cups distilled white vinegar (or cider vinegar), 3 cups water, 1 1/2 cups sugar, 1 1/2 tablespoon sea salt in a large saucepan. Bring to a boil and stir until the salt and sugar are dissolved. Let boil for 2 minutes. Remove from the heat. Pour over jar of vegetables.

LAYERED VEGETABLE

2 cups basmati rice, 3 cardamon pods, 1 bay leaf, 1 cinnamon stick, 1 tsp salt (RICE)

Preheat oven to 400F. Rince rice 3-4 times. Bring pan of water to boil & add rice, spices, and salt. Boil until just tender – about 10 mins. Drain well then keep warm. In baking tray toss sliced vegetables with garlic, salt & spices. Roast for 15-20 mins until just soft.

6 cups thick sliced mixed vegetables, 2 tbsp veg oil, 1 large onion, 3 cloves garlic, 3 cardamon pods, 3 cloves, 1 tsp ground coriander, 1 tsp ground cumin, 1 tsp ground cinnamon, 1 tsp salt, 1 tbsp melted butter

PILAF

Spread half of vegetables evenly in 9 x 12 inch baking dish. Then spread half of rice evenly on top then rest of veg then remainder of rice. Drizzle melted butter over this layer then cover with foil. Bake in oven for 10-15 mins. Serve with yogurt or raita

250g dried wheat noodles

1 tbsp Marigold boullion

handful dried rice noodles

RICE NOODL

1 lime cut into thick wedges

chilli oil to taste

NOODLE

marigold Bouillo powder

3 medium onions minced

2 eggs

1 cm root ginger

VEGETABLE OIL

FISH SAUCE

PAPRIKA

2 tbsp sweet paprika

4 tbsp vegetable oil

2 tbsp fish sauce

Mi Mi's BURMESE Coconut
Ohn-no Khao Swè

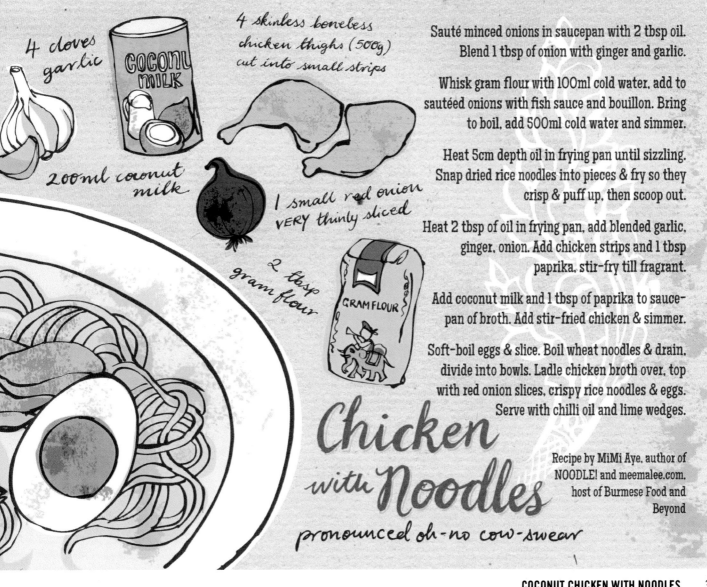

4 cloves garlic

COCONUT MILK

200ml coconut milk

4 skinless boneless chicken thighs (500g) cut into small strips

1 small red onion VERY thinly sliced

2 tbsp gram flour

GRAM FLOUR

Sauté minced onions in saucepan with 2 tbsp oil. Blend 1 tbsp of onion with ginger and garlic.

Whisk gram flour with 100ml cold water, add to sautéed onions with fish sauce and bouillon. Bring to boil, add 500ml cold water and simmer.

Heat 5cm depth oil in frying pan until sizzling. Snap dried rice noodles into pieces & fry so they crisp & puff up, then scoop out.

Heat 2 tbsp of oil in frying pan, add blended garlic, ginger, onion. Add chicken strips and 1 tbsp paprika, stir-fry till fragrant.

Add coconut milk and 1 tbsp of paprika to saucepan of broth. Add stir-fried chicken & simmer.

Soft-boil eggs & slice. Boil wheat noodles & drain, divide into bowls. Ladle chicken broth over, top with red onion slices, crispy rice noodles & eggs. Serve with chilli oil and lime wedges.

Chicken with Noodles

pronounced oh-no cow-swear

Recipe by MiMi Aye, author of NOODLE! and meemalee.com, host of Burmese Food and Beyond

COCHIN coconut
PRAWN CURRY

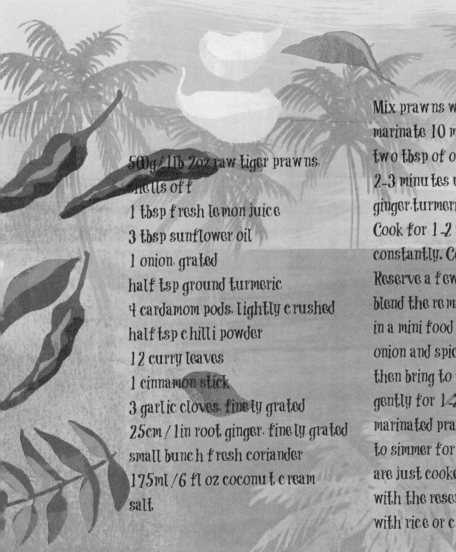

500g/1lb 2oz raw tiger prawns, shells off

1 tbsp fresh lemon juice

3 tbsp sunflower oil

1 onion, grated

half tsp ground turmeric

4 cardamom pods, lightly crushed

half tsp chilli powder

12 curry leaves

1 cinnamon stick

3 garlic cloves, finely grated

25cm/1in root ginger, finely grated

small bunch fresh coriander

175ml/6 fl oz coconut cream

salt

Mix prawns with the lemon juice and leave to marinate 10 mins. Heat a heavy-based pan with two tbsp of oil and then add onion. Cook for 2-3 minutes until soft, then add garlic and ginger, turmeric, curry leafs & whole spices. Cook for 1-2 minutes until fragrant, stirring constantly. Cook for another 1-2 minutes. Reserve a few coriander sprigs for garnish and blend the remainder with the coconut cream in a mini food processor. Stir into pan with the onion and spice mixture until well combined, then bring to the boil. Reduce heat and simmer gently for 1-2 minutes, then stir in the marinated prawns. Season with salt. Continue to simmer for 1-2 minutes until the prawns are just cooked through. Garnish the curry with the reserved coriander sprigs and serve with rice or chapattis.

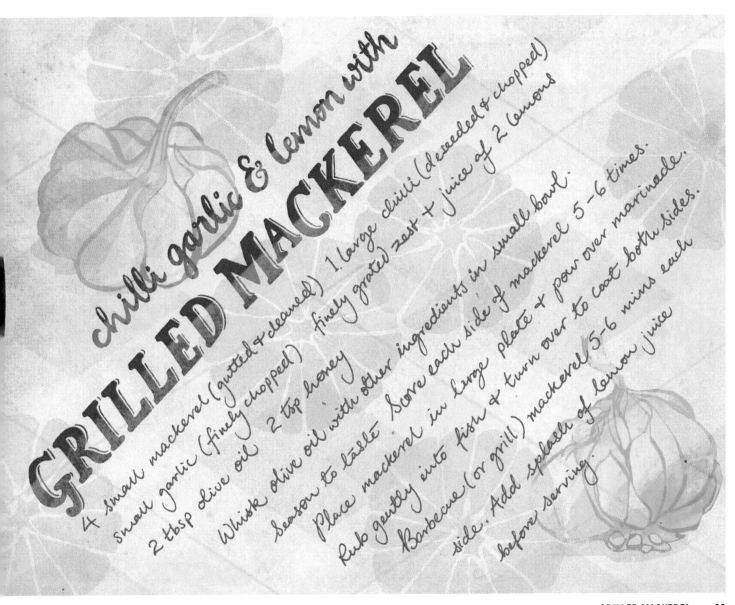

GRILLED MACKEREL

chilli garlic & lemon with

4 small mackerel (gutted & cleaned) 1 large chilli (deseeded & chopped)
small garlic (finely chopped) finely grated zest + juice of 2 lemons
2 tbsp olive oil   2 tsp honey

Whisk olive oil with other ingredients in small bowl.
Season to taste. Score each side of mackerel 5-6 times.
Place mackerel in large plate & pour over marinade.
Rub gently into fish & turn over to coat both sides.
Barbecue (or grill) mackerel 5-6 mins each
side. Add splash of lemon juice
before serving.

Four ~~Seasons~~ Persons Pizza

1 tsp caster sugar

1 tsp salt

any pizza toppings of choice

300ml lukewarm water

2 tbsp olive oil

Mix flour & salt in mixing bowl & make well in middle. In a jug mix yeast sugar & olive oil into water then pour into well. Using a wooden spoon mix until its all comes together.

Knead until you have a soft dough – about 5 mins. Place in large bowl & cover with damp cloth. Leave in warm place for 1 hour to rise.

Knead dough for 1 min then divide into two balls. Roll out each one until 0.5 cm thick. Place in oiled pan or flat baking sheet

passater

500g strong white flow

1g dried yeast sachet

Spread passata thinly over dough season with salt & pepper and dried oregano.

Sprinkle with diced mozerella. Spread toppings of choice onto each quarter of pizza. Bake in oven 250C for 8-10 mins.

This is what we do in our house so we can all have our favourite toppings

Apple &

2 bramley apple, peeled, cored & chopped

50g brown sugar

200g blackberries

50g wholemeal flour

50g plain flour

40g butter chopped into cubes

½ tsp ground cinnamon

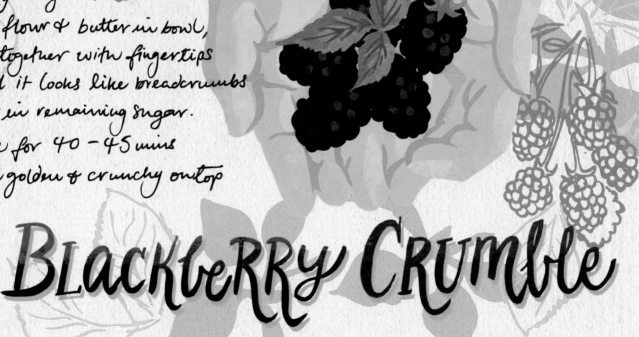

Preheat oven to 180°C
Put apples in oven proof
dish with blackberries
10g of sugar & cinnamon
Put flour & butter in bowl,
rub together with fingertips
until it looks like breadcrumbs
Stir in remaining sugar.
Bake for 40 - 45 mins
until golden & crunchy on top

BLACKBERRY CRUMBLE

125g unsalted butter
100g muscovado sugar
4 tbsp golden syrup
325g plain flour
1 tsp bicarbonate of soda
2 tsp ground ginger

Preheat the oven to 170C.
Melt the butter, sugar and syrup.
Sieve the flour, bicarbonate of soda
and ginger into a bowl. Stir the melted
ingredients to make a stiff dough.
Turn out onto a floured surface and
roll to a thickness of 5mm. Cut out shapes.
Place the shapes on baking trays lined with
greaseproof paper. Bake for 9-10 mins.
When completely cool, decorate with the icing.

CHRISTMAS gingerbread

Kids love rolling and cutting out the dough. And of course decorating the biscuits and hanging them on the tree.

Freshly Brewed

COFFEE with

FREE refills 15¢

4 eggs
2 cups sugar
1/4 cup of coffee diluted in 3/4 cup of hot water
1 cup oil
2 scoops vanilla sugar
2 cups flour
2 teaspoons baking powder
1/4 cup cocoa

Coffee BUNDT CAKE

Beat the eggs and sugar until fluffy. Add the coffee and oil. In a separate bowl, mix the dry ingredients. Add to the wet ingredients. Pour into a greased and floured bundt pan and Bake at 350 for (approximately) 45 minutes, until a toothpick inserted comes out clean.

Glaze:
3 teaspoons coffee dissolved in 2 tbsp boiling water
2 tablespoons oil
2 cups of confectioners sugar

Mix coffee, oil and confectioners sugar. Drizzle the glaze over cooled cake.

FESTIVE

Cupcakes

For the frosting
85g unsalted butter, softened
1 tsp vanilla extract
200g icing sugar, sifted
Natural red and green food colouring

Decorate with Chritmassy sweets, chocolate stars and sprinkles.

For the cakes

280g self-raising flour
175g golden caster sugar
175g unsalted butter, very soft
150g pot fat-free natural yogurt
1 tsp vanilla extract
3 eggs

Method

Heat oven to 190C/170 fan/gas 5. Line a 12-hole muffin tin with cake cases. Put all the cake ingredients into a bowl and mix with whisk until smooth. Spoon the mix into the cases, bake for 25 mins until golden. Cool on a wire rack.

For the frosting, beat the butter, vanilla extract and icing sugar until pale and creamy and completely combined. Divide frosting and colour with red and green food colouring. Pipe onto the cakes using a star-shaped nozzle. Decorate with sweets and sprinkles.

lemon & sweet tea

Slice lemons & place in molds, then pour sweet tea over them

Place cucumber slices in each mold then pour (2 cups) lemonade over them

cucumber & lemonade

blueberry & yogurt

mix 1½ cup greek yogurt with honey (to taste) Stir in 1 cup blueberries Pour into molds.

cherry & lime

Blend 1 cup cranberry juice with 1 cup frozen cherries, 1 tsp lime juice & zest of lime until smooth

strawberry & apple

Blend 6 strawberries with 4oz fresh apple juice. Pour into mold

Place 3 raspberries in each mold then pour (2 cups) lemonade over them

FRUITY FILLED POPSICLES

raspberry & pink lemonade

all recipes make 4-6 popsicles

add stick & pop back in freezer

freeze for 30-60 mins then

add orange slices to mold & pour in peach juice

watermelon & cucumber

orange & peach

blend watermelon & cucumber together, strain then pour into molds.

Blend 1 lb ripe peaches with 1/4 cup fresh orange juice Add sugar to taste

cheats
(or child friendly)

KIWI
& Berry
PAVLOVA

With or without a child helping you

Place meringue case on serving dish

Whip cream until fluffy and generously spread across the top of pavlova

Place fruit across top of cream in pretty pattern

1 large bought meringue shell
1 cup heavy cream for whipping
1 cup berries of choice
2 kiwi fruit peeled and sliced

For the cakes
4oz unsalted butter,
4oz caster sugar
2 free-range eggs
4oz self-raising flour
5oz raspberries
6 passion fruit, sieved pulp
a little milk

For the icing
1lb 1½oz icing sugar
5½oz butter
1 vanilla pod, seeds only
2 drops pink food colouring
50ml/1¾oz milk

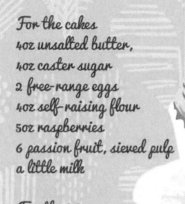

Preheat the oven to 350 F. Beat the butter and sugar in a bowl. Add the eggs & beat well. Fold the flour, raspberries and passion fruit pulp into the mixture.

AMORE LOVE

I ♥ you

Add a little milk, as necessary. Divide the mixture among 12 paper cases then bake for 20 minutes. Remove from the oven and set aside to cool. For the icing, using an electric whisk, cream the icing sugar and butter together until light and fluffy. Whisk in the vanilla seeds and food colouring. Spoon the icing into a piping bag & pipe the icing over the cake.

Passionfruit & Raspberry CUPCAKES

3/4 cup/150g granulated sugar

1 pound/460g plums pitted & chopped

taste of fruit

Seasons full of mists and mellow fruitfulness,
Close bosom friend of the maturing sun;

J. Keats

PLUM JAM

Combine plums + sugar in bowl. Let them sit for 1 hour.
Place fruit in large skillet, over medium high heat.
Stirring regularly bring fruit to gentle boil.
Starts to thicken 10 to 12 mins.
Its done when jam starts to stick to side of pan a lot!
Remove jam from heat + funnel into sterilised jars.

let's bake

SCONES

Preheat the oven to 220C/425F/Gas 7. Put flour and baking powder in large bowl. Add butter and rub in until the mixture resembles breadcrumbs. Stir in sugar and sultanas. Beat egg in measuring jug. Make up to 100ml with the milk, then set aside a tablespoon for glazing scones. Gradually add egg and milk to the dry ingredients, stirring until it's a soft dough. Turn mixture out and roll out until 2cm/¾in thick. Use a 4cm/1½in fluted cutter to stamp out the scones. Arrange scones on the greased baking trays and brush the tops with remaining milk. Bake for 8-10 minutes, or until risen and golden-brown. Cool on wire rack .To serve, cut each scone in half and top with strawberry jam and clotted or whipped cream.

250g/9oz self-raising flour
1 rounded tsp baking powder
40g/1½oz softened butter
25g/1oz caster sugar
1 large free-range egg
75g (21/2oz) sultanas
about 100ml/3½fl oz milk

Victoria Sandwich

4 free-range eggs 225g/8oz caster sugar,
225g/8oz self-raising flour 2 tsp baking powder
225g/8oz soft butter plus little extra to grease tins

To serve
good-quality strawberry jam
whipped double cream

Preheat the oven to 180C/ 350F/ Gas 4. Grease and line 2 x 20cm/ 8in sandwich tins. Break the eggs into a large mixing bowl, then add the sugar, flour, baking powder and butter. Mix everything together until well combined. Divide the mixture evenly between the tins. Place the tins on the middle shelf of the oven and bake for 25 minutes. Remove them from the oven and set aside to cool completely. To assemble the cake, place one cake upside down onto a plate and spread it with plenty of jam, then the whipped cream. Top with the second cake, top-side up.

THEY DRAW & COOK™

**The Most Gorgeous Cookbook Ever
by Ohn Mar Win**

Conceived, designed and produced
by Studio SSS and Ohn Mar Win

STUDIO SSS, LLC
Nate Padavick & Salli Swindell
studiosss.tumblr.com

OHN MAR WIN
ohnmarwin.com

Conversions

Common Measurement Equivalents

3 TS = 1 TBS = 1/2 FL OZ
2 TS = 1 FL OZ
4 TS = 2 FL OZ = 1/4 C
8 TBS = 4 FL OZ = 1/2 C
16 TBS = 8 FL OZ = 1 C
16 FL OZ = 2 C = 1 PT
32 FL OZ = 4 C = 2 PT = 1 QT
128 FL OZ = 16 C = 8 PT = 4 QT = 1 G

Volume

1 TS	5 ML
1 TBS	15 ML
1/4 C	59 ML
1 C	236 ML
1 PT	472 ML
1 QT	944 ML
1 G	3.8 L

Length

1 IN	2.54 CM
4 IN	10 CM
6 IN	5 CM
8 IN	20 CM
9 IN	23 CM
10 IN	25 CM
12 IN	30 CM
13 IN	33 CM

Weight/Mass

1/4 OZ	7 G
1/3 OZ	10 G
1/2 OZ	14 G
1 OZ	28 G
2 OZ	57 G
3 OZ	85 G
4 OZ	113 G
5 OZ	142 G
6 OZ	170 G
7 OZ	198 G
8 OZ	227 G
9 OZ	255 G
10 OZ	284 G
11 OZ	312 G
12 OZ	340 G
13 OZ	369 G
14 OZ	397 G
15 OZ	425 G
16 OZ	454 G

Oven Temperatures

300°F	150°C
325°F	165°C
350°F	180°C
375°F	190°C
400°F	200°C
425°F	220°C
450°F	230°C
475°F	245°C

Helpful Formulas

Tablespoons x 14.79 = Milliliters
Cups x 0.236 = Liters
Ounces x 28.35 = Grams
Degrees F − 32 x 5 ÷ 9 = Degrees C
Inches x 2.54 = Centimeters

Made in the USA
Columbia, SC
30 October 2021